D1152932

WOMEN'S RIGHTS

Changing Attitudes 1900-2000

Kaye Stearman

PRODUCED IN ASSOCIATION WITH
AMNESTY INTERNATIONAL

an imprint of Hodder Children's Books

Twentieth Century Issues series

Censorship
Crime and Punishment
Medical Ethics
Poverty
Racism
Women's Rights

(handwritten: Women's Rights / Women's Liberation / World History 20th)

Produced for Wayland Publishers Limited by Discovery Books Limited, Unit 3, 37 Watling Street, Leintwardine, Shropshire SY7 0LW, England

Editor: Patience Coster
Series editor: Alex Woolf
Series design: Mind's Eye Design, Lewes
Consultants: Dr Kate Nash and Amnesty International

First published in Great Britain in 1999
by Wayland Publishers Ltd
Reprinted in 2000 by Hodder Wayland,
an imprint of Hodder Children's Books

Acknowledgements

The author would like to thank Frances Connelly and David Doughan and other staff at the Fawcett Library, the National Library of Women, London.

This title produced in association with Amnesty International UK.
Amnesty International is a worldwide human rights movement which is independent of any government, political faction, ideology, economic interest or religious creed. (See page 62).

The views expressed in this publication do not necessarily reflect the views of Amnesty International.

Picture acknowledgements

Amnesty International 47, 54; Associated Press/Topham 22; Corbis 52 (Dean Conger); Corbis-Bettmann 29; Corbis-Bettman/UPI 36, 38, 43; Mary Evans/Fawcett Library 10, 11; Mary Evans/Fawcett Library (courtesy of Smith College Library) 18 (top); Mary Evans Picture Library 6, 9, 16; Hulton-Deutsch Collection/Corbis 13; Hulton Getty Picture Collection 21, 28, 42; Impact 45 (Jeremy Nicholl), 50 (Alice Mason); Library of Congress/Corbis 8; Pacha/Corbis 55; Panos Pictures 4 (Ron Giling), 30 (Catherine Platt), 49 (Oliver Garcia), 51 (Zed Nelson); Popperfoto 7, 15, 24, 31, 32, 33, 35; Popperfoto/Reuter 39, 44, 46, 57 (Corinne Dufka), 58 (Dylan Martinez); Tony Stone Images 59; Superstock 27; Topham Picturepoint 5, 12, 20, 26, 40, 41, 48, 56; United Press International 17; UPI/Corbis-Bettmann 23; Wayland Picture Library 18 (bottom, illustration by Strube, Daily Express 1927, courtesy of the Centre for the Study of Cartoons and Caricature, University of Kent at Canterbury), 25.

Cover: main picture shows a women's pro-choice rally in the USA (Topham Picturepoint); black-and-white pictures show, top to bottom, the arrest of a suffragette in London (Topham Picturepoint); Women's Liberation Movement in New York City, 1970s (Popperfoto); and a woman with her children in southern Africa (UNEP/Traudi Riegger/Topham).

CONTENTS

AN UNEQUAL WORLD

Baby comes too! Learning to read and write will open new opportunities for this woman and her children.

The twentieth century has been a period of rapid and far-reaching change for many women worldwide. But for all this progress, life for women in some parts of the world remains harsh. Even where women have experienced great advances, there are still some similarities between their lives today and the lives of women in 1900. This book charts the course of the movement for women's rights over the last hundred years and looks at how the dramatic social, economic, technological and medical changes of the century have been linked with the revolution in women's lives.

During the eighteenth and nineteenth centuries, attempts were made to define and extend people's human rights. But most of these struggles ignored or denied the rights of half the human race – women. The twentieth century has been marked by struggles to bring to women the full range of human rights. 'Women's rights' means equal rights for women and men, but it goes beyond equality – it means recognizing the particular problems and difficulties confronting women and finding ways to overcome these barriers. 'Women's rights' means seeking opportunities for women to use their skills and experience and allowing them to participate as equals in society.

CITIZENSHIP RIGHTS

Political and legal rights are rights guaranteed by governments and legal systems. The right to vote and stand for election, to be treated equally and fairly, to speak freely and to use the law to support our rights – all these are our rights as citizens. In many countries these citizenship rights are still denied to women – and to men also. But just as important are economic and social rights that enable people to use political and civil rights and participate in society. These include the right to food and shelter, to family life, to a decent standard of living and to education and employment.

During the course of the twentieth century, women's rights have included all these rights and many more. Women's rights over their own bodies have been of particular importance. In much of Europe during the nineteenth century women were regarded as 'chattels' – the property of their husbands or fathers. Women were sometimes looked down on as 'minors', in other words as children without rights or responsibilities. In some countries today, women are still placed in these categories and are prevented from making basic decisions about their own lives.

In nineteenth-century America, women's rights campaigners organized to demand citizenship rights.

KEY MOMENT

Woman scientist makes medical breakthrough

Marie Curie (1867-1934) showed that women could excel in science. Born in Poland, she studied physics and mathematics at the Sorbonne University in Paris, France. With her husband Pierre Curie, she discovered two new radioactive elements, polonium and radium, later used in X-rays. In 1903, the Curies shared the Nobel Prize for physics. In 1911, Marie Curie was awarded a second Nobel Prize in chemistry.

OPINION

'We little dreamed when we began this contest that half a century later we would be compelled to leave the finish of the battle to another generation of women.'
Susan B Anthony, American women's rights campaigner, 1898.

The fight for women's rights started long before 1900. The French Revolution of 1789-99 overthrew the established order: revolutionaries declared the new 'Rights of Man'. A French woman, Olympe de Gouges, and an English woman, Mary Wollstonecraft, argued that these rights should also apply to women. In the nineteenth century, revolutionary political movements in Europe sparked demands for greater equality.

In the USA, the anti-slavery movement inspired demands for equal rights for women. After the abolition of slavery in 1865, voting rights were extended to all citizens. But the term 'citizens' referred only to men – women were excluded from citizenship. For fifty years, Susan B Anthony and Elizabeth Cady Stanton campaigned for women to have the vote. Although both women lived to see the new century, they died long before American women could vote on equal terms with men.

The nineteenth century was a century of change. Industrialization and improved transport and communications changed the pattern of people's working lives. A few exceptional women were gaining an education and entering public life. While the nations of South America gained independence from Spain and Portugal, other European powers such as Britain, France and Germany seized control of much of Africa and Asia. It was this world, with all its change and inequalities, that laid the foundation for the new women's rights movement.

Inspired by the 'Rights of Man', Mary Wollstonecraft (left) argued that human rights should be extended to women.

A NEW WOMAN FOR A NEW CENTURY

In the 1890s, large numbers of women became involved in women's rights issues for the first time. Young, independent women started questioning conventional ideas about marriage, sex and family life as well as inequalities in women's legal and political rights. In 1894, the term 'new woman' began to be used in novels and magazines. In 1895, another new term appeared – 'feminist'.

There was widespread discussion of both terms. Supporters of the 'new woman' rejected common ideas of women as dependent and passive, inferior to their brothers and obedient to their husbands. Instead they promoted the ideal woman as independent and active, a woman who made her own decisions which often included the rejection of marriage as a degrading institution. A 'feminist' was a person (woman or man) who supported more equal rights and fairer treatment for women.

OPINION

'We have not wrecked the railroad nor corrupted the legislatures, nor done many unholy things that men have done, but then we must remember that we have not had the chance.'
Jane Addams, US feminist and social reformer, 1911.

The 'new woman' wore clothing to promote an independent, active life and rejected conventional ideas of domestic duty.

By the early twentieth century, many working-class women worked in factories, earning and spending their own money. The photo shows women mill workers at a factory in Spain.

Many people were deeply opposed to giving greater freedom and rights to women. They found the new ideas shocking and revolutionary, claiming that they were 'against all the tenets of God and Man'. But others welcomed new ideas and attitudes. And there were many differences of opinion among feminists themselves. Many 'new women' wanted new types of relationships and greater personal freedoms, including sexual freedom. However, other feminists disliked these ideas, and believed that their aims would be achieved by campaigning for specific political and legal rights.

Campaigns were launched for better education for girls, to reform unfair marriage, divorce and property laws and to remove barriers in education or employment – issues of particular concern to middle-class women. Increasingly, campaigns also embraced issues in the lives of working-class women, such as poverty, poor housing, low wages and domestic violence. Some feminists worked with trade unions and co-operatives recruiting women, or with socialist parties that were sending their first representatives to parliaments.

THE RIGHT TO VOTE

However, as the twentieth century dawned, one issue came to the fore. This was women's suffrage – the right of women to vote in national, state and local elections on the same terms as men. Campaigners for suffrage became known as 'suffragists'.

In most countries in 1900 women could not vote in elections or be elected as representatives in parliaments or councils. In itself, this is not surprising. Most men were also denied political rights. Governments were run by small groups of men who had inherited power or who had seized it by force. In a few countries, mostly in northern Europe and North America, politics was becoming more open to ordinary citizens. But only men were considered to be 'full citizens'.

In 1900 the only country in which women could vote was New Zealand, where voting rights had been granted to women in 1893. Australia followed in 1902, although women in some Australian states had been able to vote before that date. By the 1890s, New Zealand and Australia had strong trade unions,

KEY MOMENT

Women vote in Europe
In 1905, revolution broke out in St Petersburg and spread to many parts of the Russian Empire, including the grand duchy of Finland. Although the revolution was defeated, popular pressure resulted in the Russian government giving the Finns their own parliament. Members were elected by universal suffrage – the first time women were allowed to vote in any European country.

Although women were expected to hold the household together, they were still denied the right to vote.

KEY MOMENT

Direct action in Britain
In 1906, in London, Christabel Pankhurst and Annie Kenny of the WSPU interrupted an election meeting addressed by Sir Edward Grey, the Home Secretary, to ask: 'Will the Liberal government give votes to working women?'. They were arrested when they spat at the policemen escorting them from the building. Their court appearance and punishment of seven days' imprisonment gained enormous publicity and marked the start of increased militancy.

growing Labour parties and the beginnings of a welfare state. Although women had to organize and argue for the vote, women's suffrage was accepted relatively early as a fact of political life.

However, in most countries, supporting women's rights was highly controversial. Opponents saw votes for women as a dangerous step; some people thought that it would destroy family relationships or lead to the collapse of society. It was difficult to bring about change through rational argument and peaceful campaigning. Nevertheless, suffragists worked hard to convince powerful men in government to give women voting rights.

THE SUFFRAGETTE MOVEMENT

In Britain, women followed an increasingly militant path after the formation of the Women's Social and Political Union in 1903. The WSPU, as it became known, was the creation of Emmeline Pankhurst and her daughter Christabel. It used high-profile, direct-action campaigns to focus attention on the cause.

British suffragettes march in the 'Great Procession' of 18 June 1910. Here male supporters carry the banner of women hunger strikers.

SUFFRAGETTES
WHO HAVE NEVER
BEEN KISSED

The subsequent arrest and imprisonment of demonstrators, who were dubbed 'suffragettes', generated a huge amount of publicity, and thousands of women flocked to support the campaign.

Suffragettes were frequently ridiculed as plain and humourless women, rejected by men. In fact, most had husbands and families.

The WSPU gradually became more militant. Groups of women chained themselves to the Ladies' Gallery in the Houses of Parliament, put acid in poll boxes, burned letters in post boxes and broke shop windows in order to court arrest. Once imprisoned, many women went on hunger strike and were forcibly fed by prison officials, causing widespread outrage. In 1913 one suffragette, Emily Wilding Davison, died after attempting to stop the king's horse at the Derby races.

The WSPU was a relatively small movement, increasingly dominated by the Pankhursts. Many feminists disapproved of their militancy, considering such tactics as undignified and class-based – working-class women without money or servants could not risk their families' welfare by going to prison. However, thousands of women joined more moderate groups, such as the National Union of Women's Suffrage Societies. Here they participated in ordered, peaceful demonstrations with colourful banners, plays and songs, although even peaceful demonstrations faced violence from political opponents and the police.

> **OPINION**
>
> 'Equal say will enable women to get equal pay.' Mallee Schepps, US trade union organizer, 1912.

In the USA, the National Women's Suffrage Association aimed to change the US Constitution. From 1878, an amendment extending voting rights to women was regularly presented to Congress in Washington. Each time, it was ignored or rejected by the all-male Congress. However, some state governments were more progressive. In 1869, Wyoming became the first US territory to grant votes to women. By 1915, fifteen states had followed Wyoming's example.

The US state of Wyoming was the first to grant women the vote. This scene from 1888 shows women queuing to vote in the town of Cheyenne.

Such slow progress did not satisfy the most determined campaigners. Inspired by the activities of British suffragettes, American women became increasingly outspoken. Instead of mass arrests, they used imaginative publicity to make their point, exploiting the new mass media of radio, telephones and public advertising. Suffragists spoke at venues such as state and country fairs and adult education classes. They forged links with immigrant women, publishing materials in Italian and Yiddish, and supported women's trade unions. Black women also participated in suffrage activities, linking women's rights to the fight for racial equality.

By 1914, when the First World War broke out, the suffragist movement had become international. However, only one European country, Finland, had granted women voting rights. Despite its failures, the struggle for women's suffrage remains of historical importance. In many countries 'votes for women' became the first mass campaign by women for women. The 'direct action' campaigning used by the suffragettes influenced other political campaigns throughout the century. But it was the upheaval caused by war and revolutions that brought new possibilities and rights for women. .

OPINION

'We woman suffragists have a great mission – the greatest mission the world has ever known. It is to free half the human race, and through that freedom to save the rest.'
Emmeline Pankhurst, British suffragette, 1912.

WOMEN IN WAR AND PEACE

In August 1914, war was declared in Europe. On one side were the empires of Germany, Austria-Hungary and the Ottomans (Turks). On the other side were the French, British and Russian empires, joined in 1917 by the USA. Women's lives were profoundly affected by the conflict of the First World War and the uneasy peace that followed.

ON HER THEIR LIVES DEPEND

WOMEN MUNITION WORKERS

Enrol at once

The British government urged women to support the war effort by volunteering to work in munitions factories.

At the beginning, many people welcomed the war. On both sides women's rights organizations halted suffrage campaigns, arguing that women should direct their energies towards the war effort. Many women's rights campaigners had seen their cause as international; now nationalism came to the fore. Some women organized against the war. Many more felt that they had no alternative but to accept the situation.

Food shortages created great hardships, especially for poor city women who had to spend more time finding and preparing what food was available. Later, essential goods were rationed but quality was often poor. As families lost their main breadwinners to the military machine, so more women had to find paid work.

Before the war, women's work had already been changing. In addition to domestic service and factory work, women had joined the growing white-collar work force as shop assistants, typists, clerks, telephone operators and postal workers. With war, the shortage of men meant that women took jobs in public transport and essential industry, like munitions factories. In Germany in 1917, over 700,000 women worked in heavy industry – six times more than in 1913.

MORE WORK FOR LESS PAY

Women became drivers, plumbers, electricians, engineers – even police officers and undertakers – all traditionally seen as 'male jobs'. Other women served as civilian or military nurses. They worked long hours in often dangerous conditions. Although women were doing men's work, they were paid much less than men. In addition, they still had to undertake their unpaid work in the home.

By the time peace was declared in November 1918, people's lives had changed forever. The pre-war order had been destroyed, empires had collapsed, and millions of people were living as homeless refugees. Several countries saw revolutionary uprisings, although none but the revolution in Russia lasted more than a few months. Governments everywhere were forced to acknowledge the new situation.

Women's suffrage, which had previously been so controversial, underwent a dramatic shift. Norway and Denmark (both neutral nations) allowed women to vote in 1913 and 1915 respectively, and revolutionary Russia gave women the vote in 1918. New nations such as Austria, Czechoslovakia and Poland, born from the break-up of old empires, also introduced women's suffrage.

Women's new and visible roles during the war had helped to change entrenched attitudes. Some governments used the vote to reward women for their war efforts. In Canada, the vote was given to army nurses in 1917 and to female relatives of soldiers in 1918. In 1919 it was extended to all women. British women over the age of thirty got the vote in 1918, but it was another ten years before women could vote on the same terms as men, at the age of twenty-one. US women finally got the vote in 1920.

In Britain, women over thirty gained equal voting rights in 1918. Holding a baby and surrounded by her children, a British woman casts her first vote.

BRAVE NEW WORLD

OPINION

'One of the first fruits of the first parliament elected partly by women voters has been this Pre-War Practices Act which, without once mentioning the word 'woman' or 'female' has the effect of legally excluding women from nearly every department of skilled industry except a few trades traditionally their own.'
Eleanor Rathbone, British feminist, 1920.

In the 1920s, fashionable women wore male clothing and bobbed their hair.

During the 1920s there were dramatic social changes. Women looked, dressed and behaved differently. Heavy, restrictive clothing gave way to lighter materials, casual styles and shorter skirts. Long hair was replaced by bob-cuts and perms. Young women took up new dances, like the charleston, and participated in sports. They flocked to cinemas and, especially in America, bought new consumer goods, like refrigerators and vacuum cleaners.

But many of the opportunities which had opened to women during the war were now closed again. Most people felt that men should be the main bread-winners, although it was generally accepted that single women and widows had a right to paid work. In Britain, the Pre-War Practices Act barred women from many jobs and married women were barred from jobs in the civil service, teaching and medicine. High unemployment levels during the Depression of the 1930s further limited women's work opportunities.

Although women could now vote, politics seemed to offer them little. A few exceptional women – some of whom championed women's rights – were elected to parliaments, but they made little impact. Some feminists argued that equality in the work place

SACHA
ZALIOUK

didn't mean much to most women, the majority of whom were wives and mothers. They said that women needed society to recognize and support them in these roles.

As a result, many feminists looked away from the world of paid employment. They campaigned for welfare measures, such as child benefit for mothers and pensions for widows, as well as legal reforms in divorce and child custody and improved status for unmarried mothers. However, inequalities continued and economic conditions, especially for poor women, remained hard.

Dancing the charleston became a symbol of the new freedom of movement.

OPINION

'Women are demanding more kinds of food, more leisure, more athletics and sports, more education, more travel, more art, more entertainment, more music, more civic improvement, better landscaping and city planning, more literature, more social graces, more social freedom and more cosmopolitan polish and smartness.'
Christine Frederick, US journalist, 1929.

Margaret Sanger (above) pioneered birth control clinics in the USA.

More controversially, some women began to promote more open and positive attitudes towards sexuality and contraception. They urged that young people should receive accurate information on sex, and that married women should have access to birth control. Open discussion on these ideas was opposed by most governments and churches and was often subject to censorship. But despite these restrictions, family sizes fell. In the 1920s in Britain and Germany the two-child family became the new norm.

During the 1920s and 1930s women's rights issues took various directions. Some women worked through the new League of Nations for international action on women's rights. Their experiences of war and fear of future wars led many to support international campaigns for peace and disarmament. These hopes were not fulfilled: by 1939, the world was again at war.

KEY MOMENT

Breakthrough in birth control

In 1916, Margaret Sanger (1879-1965) opened the first birth control clinic in the USA to assist poor working-class women escape unwanted and unsafe childbearing. She was arrested and jailed but later won her case and went on to found 300 similar clinics. She later founded the International Planned Parenthood Federation and supported the development of the birth control pill.

The ghost of a pre-war suffragette looks on in disgust at a fashionable flapper in this British cartoon from 1927.

SHADE OF OLD MILITANT: "So this is what I fought for!"

REVOLUTION AND REPRESSION

In a few countries, governments developed policies and passed laws on women. These laws reflected the ideologies (political beliefs) of governments – their views on what women should be and do – rather than the demands of women themselves.

The First World War had brought Russia close to collapse. In March 1917, the desperate economic situation drove women to riot in the streets. The revolution that followed led to the overthrow of the monarchy, a takeover by the Communist Party and a bitter civil war. Many women saw the Russian Revolution as a revolution for women – one that would transform their lives for the better.

NEW GAINS IN RUSSIA

The new government in Russia granted women the right to vote. Marriage was made a civil contract rather than a religious ceremony, recognizing women and men as equal partners and making provision for divorce and maintenance payments for children. The law allowed abortion on demand, equal pay for women and men, and sixteen weeks maternity leave on full pay. State nurseries and collective kitchens were set up. As over eighty per cent of women could not read, women received special attention in campaigns to increase literacy and improve educational opportunities.

These policies benefited women and helped to raise their status. However, it was difficult to improve women's lives during wartime and the harsh years that followed. The principle of equal pay was not enforced and most women remained in low-paid, unskilled jobs.

> ### KEY MOMENT
>
> **Riots in Petrograd**
> The actions of ordinary women in St Petersburg (then called Petrograd) led directly to the Russian Revolution. By early 1917 the transport system had broken down and food and fuel failed to reach the city. Tired of queuing for hours for bread, women took to the streets and attacked the city's bakeries. A revolutionary overheard one typist say to another: 'Do you know, I think it's the beginning of a revolution?'.

In the Soviet Union women, like this group in 1937, undertook heavy work on giant new collective farms.

Nurseries were not available for all children and collective kitchens soon closed. The right to vote meant little as the new Soviet Union was a one-party state and few women reached the higher levels of government.

By 1930, the dictator Josef Stalin had taken complete control. Women's rights became secondary to the quest for economic growth. Women were expected to work alongside men in the giant new factories and farms, then spend hours queuing for food, then tackle the housework and childcare. The number of abortions, the only effective form of birth control available, rose. In 1936, Stalin made abortions illegal. Instead, women were rewarded if they had large families.

NATIONAL SOCIALISM

In Germany a similar process was taking place, whereby women's rights were being dictated by government policies. Following Germany's surrender in 1918, there were months of revolutionary unrest during which many women joined political parties and trade unions. Germany's new constitution recognized women and men as equals and women could vote in elections. However, solving economic problems, such as hyper-inflation and unemployment, was seen as more urgent than women's rights. Women representatives in parliament focused on issues such as child welfare, health and education. However, many younger women experienced greater freedom and independence in their daily lives. By 1925, there were three times as many women in the new white-collar jobs than in 1907, and growing numbers in professional jobs as doctors, teachers and nurses.

In 1933 the National Socialists (Nazis), led by Adolf Hitler, were elected to government and rapidly established a dictatorship, banning other political parties and arresting, jailing and killing opponents. The Nazis were opposed to women's rights. Working women were depicted as taking jobs away from men. Josef Goebbels, Minister for Propaganda, said: 'A woman's most fitting place is in the family, and the most glorious duty she can fulfil is to present her people and her country with a child'.

A German poster from 1932 urges women to vote for the National Socialist (Nazi) Party.

Once in power, the Nazis burned and destroyed books on women's rights, sex education and family planning.

While many Germans sympathized with National Socialist ideas, the Nazis pursued their aims with a fanaticism that surprised all but their most committed followers. Books on feminism and family planning were publicly burned. Girls' education focused on domestic subjects to prepare them for motherhood. Childless couples paid high taxes while young married couples were given special loans to encourage them to have children. These measures applied only to 'racially pure' Germans – Jews, gypsies and foreigners were persecuted, and disabled or mentally-ill women were sterilized or were forced to give up their children; in some cases their children were killed.

However, while the Nazis banned married women from civil service posts and restricted the numbers of single women entering universities or professional jobs, the reality was often different. Labour shortages meant restrictions on women's work were often ignored, so many married women continued to work. By 1939, on the eve of war, more German women than ever were in paid work.

OPINION

'...organizations set out to prepare the girls for their future professions, National Socialist motherhood and war machines, either as nurses or as "defenders of the homeland". Everything about race and motherhood is taught them, as well as everything about *Eintopfgerichte* (one-pot dishes), *Ersatz* fat, the uses of slops, how to risk one's life for the cause, and first aid.' Erika Mann, author, 1939.

WOMEN IN THE FRONT LINE

Germany invaded Poland in September 1939. When Britain and France declared war on Germany a few days later, it signalled the beginning of a conflict even more devastating than the First World War. Following the occupation of neighbouring countries, German armies invaded the Soviet Union in 1941. Full-scale war between the USA and Japan began later in the same year.

The Second World War made a huge impact on women's lives and working experiences. As in the First World War, women took over many jobs formerly occupied by men. Many worked in industries vital to the war effort, others worked in civilian jobs in service areas or the professions. They participated directly, in women's branches of the armed forces or as support services.

In most countries women were recruited on a voluntary basis, with appeals to their patriotism and to support their men-folk. In Germany, young women were expected to serve in the *Arbeitsdienst* (Voluntary Labour Service) for six months or a year, as 'maids of labour' in farming or government services. The worst jobs and conditions were experienced by the millions of women and men captured by German armies and forced to work as slave labourers.

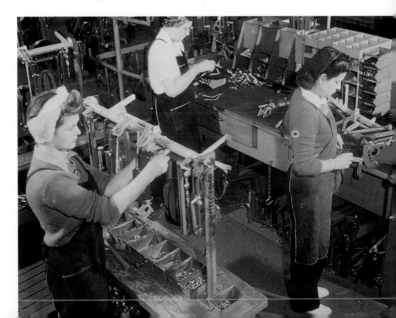

While men served with the military, huge numbers of women workers, like this group in California, took over men's jobs on the assembly lines.

NATIONAL SERVICE

OPINION

'The creature putting out incendiary bombs; hacking a way into caved-in cellars with a pick-axe; perched on the rooftop in a steel helmet; dragging furniture out of burning rooms... this sexless, brave, competent being: is it really still a woman? Does it still need protecting? Women are now beasts of burden.'
Ursula von Kardorff,
German journalist, 1944.

Women played a vital role in the defence of the Soviet Union. These women naval officers led an all-women crew.

In Britain, women joined the war effort in large numbers. Later, in 1941, registration for work was made compulsory and unmarried women aged between twenty and thirty were called for compulsory national service. By mid-1943, ninety per cent of single women and eighty per cent of married women were employed in the armed forces or industry. In the USA there was a 460 per cent increase in the number of women in heavy industry.

Governments made special efforts to support women workers. Shifts were arranged to allow women to work part-time. Day-care centres and nurseries were provided for working mothers. Although wages were often better than in peace time, women did not earn equal pay with men and many were resented by male supervisors.

For many young women, the war years were a liberating experience, the first time they had lived or travelled away from their homes and families. In Britain and the USA the war also brought greater social equality; although life was hard and sometimes dangerous, there was a common sense of unity and purpose.

Set against this was the huge danger and damage experienced by civilians. Long-range missiles and aerial bombing, developed in the 1930s, brought war directly to the cities of Europe and Asia. Women were in the front line as firewardens and rescuers. Food and fuel were rationed and women had to make the best of what little was available. Women living in areas under Nazi or Japanese occupation experienced terrible privations.

While the surrenders of Germany (May 1945) and Japan (August 1945) ended the war, in many countries daily life remained difficult and insecure. Housing was destroyed and there were food and fuel shortages. Huge numbers of men had been killed or were missing – many never returned home and many of those who did were permanently disabled. Women had to carry on as best they could amid the chaos.

As the armies disbanded and men returned home, women were encouraged to step down from their 'temporary jobs' to make way for the returning soldiers. Many were dismissed or given 'female' jobs. In the USA, eighty per cent of women who

Unlike men, at the end of their shift women war-workers had to tackle domestic duties and family responsibilities.

HOUSEWIFE 1944

The Hand that held the Hoover works the Lathe!

With no glamour of uniform, with all the burdens and responsibilities of running a home, thousands of housewives in 1944 are war-workers too. They are doing a double job. They get no medals for it. But if ever women deserved especial honour, these do. So to all war-workers who also tackle shopping queues, cooking, cleaning, mending and the hundred and one other household jobs

Salute! FROM HOOVER

Hoover users know best what improvements they would like in the post-war Hoover. Suggestions are welcome.

BY APPOINTMENT TO H.M. KING GEORGE VI AND H.M. QUEEN MARY
HOOVER LIMITED, PERIVALE, GREENFORD, MIDDLESEX

Women welcomed home their husbands, sons and brothers from the war. But the men's return saw many women losing their jobs.

had trained as shipbuilders, riveters and machinists during the war wanted to continue in these jobs. During the war, images such as 'Rosie the Riveter' promoted women as strong, capable and patriotic workers; now the public perception of these women workers altered, and they were portrayed as unfeminine and unnatural.

THE AFTERMATH OF WAR

After years of Depression and war, many women and men wanted to rebuild their lives, to settle into new homes and raise families. The US economy had been strengthened by the war and greater prosperity made people's lives easier. In Europe and Japan, life remained difficult for another decade, but by the mid-1950s ordinary people had higher living standards than before the war. Wages rose and consumer goods became widely available. Most Western countries experienced a 'baby boom'.

KEY MOMENT

The Second Sex
In 1949 a book entitled *The Second Sex* by the French philosopher Simone de Beauvoir (1908-1986) was published in France. It appeared in English translation in 1953. The book looked at many different aspects of women's history and contemporary lives and was hugely influential in the Women's Liberation movement of the 1960s and 1970s.

A general pattern emerged. Unmarried women worked in 'female' jobs, especially in the growing service industries and the caring professions, such as nursing. Upon marriage, they were expected to leave paid work and become housewives, devoting themselves to husband and children. Sometimes they returned to work, often part-time, after their children had grown, or in times of hardship. Not all countries followed this model. War losses meant that many women remained unmarried or brought up children alone. The Soviet Union had suffered the worst losses; here labour shortages combined with low wages meant that most women continued in paid work after marriage and into old age.

It is not surprising that women's rights issues were given low priority during this period. Nevertheless, there were some steps forward. In 1944, newly liberated France gave women the right to vote – ninety-six years after men. The new German constitution of 1949 gave women equal rights with men, although it took many years before all unequal laws were changed. In Britain, married women were again allowed to work in teaching and the civil service. Equally important was the new 'child benefit', which was paid directly to women rather than to their husbands.

As the 1960s dawned, the concerns about women's rights in Western countries seemed, with a few exceptions, to belong to history. However, in many countries, women's rights were seen as part of a greater issue – the independence struggle.

In the 1950s, women were encouraged to direct their energies towards homemaking and motherhood.

INDEPENDENCE STRUGGLES

In 1900, most of the world's women lived in areas dominated by foreign powers – mainly Britain and France, but also Portugal, the Netherlands, Germany, the USA and Japan. In these areas, struggles for women's rights often went hand-in-hand with struggles for national independence, especially in the fifty years between 1920 and 1970. By 1975, over a hundred new nations had gained independence.

The largest of these empires was the British Empire, and the most prized possession of the British Empire was India (present-day India, Pakistan and Bangladesh). With a few exceptions, Indian women, whether Hindu or Muslim, had low status in society and were regarded as inferior to men. Indian reformers established schools and colleges for girls and women, and campaigned against customs such as *sati* (the burning to death of Hindu widows) or *purdah* (the practice of keeping women confined indoors).

Indian reformers campaigned against sati (the burning of widows), a traditional practice graphically illustrated in the picture below.

NON-VIOLENT RESISTANCE

Mohandas Gandhi, known as the Mahatma ('a great soul'), involved huge numbers of Indian women in the struggle for independence.

From the early 1920s, Indian demands for independence from Britain grew under the leadership of Mohandas (Mahatma) Gandhi of the opposition Indian National Congress. Gandhi practised *satyagraha* – or 'truth force' – non-violent resistance using direct action tactics, some of which were similar to the methods used by British suffragettes. There were huge demonstrations, marches, fasts, and gatherings to burn British goods, eventually involving millions of people. Women flocked to join the new movement. For the first time, large numbers of women were involved in public life.

After independence in 1947, the new Indian Constitution formally recognized women's rights by stating that all people were equal before the law and that there should be no discrimination on the grounds of sex. It also stated that the government had the right to take positive action on behalf of women. However, women still faced huge difficulties in putting these new rights into action, especially poor rural women whose lives were still governed by backbreaking work and traditional restrictions.

KEY MOMENT

Civil disobedience in India

Women played a vital part in the 1930-1 civil disobedience movement, especially in western India. Women picketed liquor and cloth shops and led processions and demonstrations, including 'women-only' marches. A few became public speakers while many more gave active support behind the scenes. Sometimes women took over organizations after male leaders were imprisoned. Many women were imprisoned and others were beaten by police.

OPINION

'First we bind our feet; second, our minds are bound; third, we are inferiors and servants of our husbands.'
Girl student leader, Tientsin, northern China, 1924.

This Chinese woman was from the last generation to experience footbinding. She has never been able to walk about freely.

Women also had low status in Chinese society. They were regarded as inferior to men and had little say in family life, despite their neverending labour at home and in the fields. A woman could be forced into marriage against her will or sold to strangers. In some areas, it was traditional for young girls' feet to be bound and broken (footbinding). A few educated city women campaigned against such abuses. These women were also involved in the nationalist movement against the foreign powers – Britain, France, Germany, Japan and the USA – which controlled much of China.

In 1919, feminism and nationalism came together in the May Fourth movement when there were massive demonstrations against the Japanese takeover of Chinese territory. Women joined protests and boycotts of Japanese goods. They also demanded rights for women, including the right to vote, to education, equal marriage laws and an end to footbinding. But despite their bravery, the movement failed and traditional ideas of women again came to the fore. It was not until 1949 that a much larger movement, led by the Chinese Communist Party, finally overthrew foreign domination and brought about revolutionary changes in women's lives.

WOMEN IN COMMUNIST CHINA

In China, as in the Soviet Union, the victorious Communists promoted women's rights. The Communist Party leader, Mao Zedong said: 'Women hold up half the sky'. The new Constitution gave women equal rights in all areas of life, including land ownership for rural women. The greatest controversy came with new laws granting women equality in marriage and divorce. So many women applied for divorces that the government began to fear the breakdown of family life. After a few years the Chinese government made divorce much harder to obtain. Under the Communists many more girls attended school, and women had longer and healthier lives than ever before. But it was the government that promoted change, rather than women themselves.

In Communist China women and girls served in the
people's militia and took part in political rallies.

KEY MOMENT

Support for the Red Army

During the war against the Japanese and the civil war that followed, the Chinese Communist Party and its 'Red Army' won great support from women. Unlike other armies who raped and looted, the Communists treated women with respect. Women's associations were set up in the 'liberated areas', women were encouraged to vote and take part in village affairs and special education programs were established for women.

WAR IN ALGERIA

One of the most violent independence struggles took place in Algeria in North Africa. Algeria had been colonized by the French, and many French people had settled there. In 1947, the French promised that Muslim Algerians (Arab and Berber peoples) would be given control of their country. But this did not happen and, in 1954, the *Front de la Liberation National* (FLN) took up arms against the French.

The war that followed was extremely brutal. Women actively fought with the FLN. Some smuggled FLN leaflets, weapons and bombs under their heavy, traditional clothing – as women could venture into areas that men could not. Those who were captured were tortured, raped and sometimes killed by French troops. It was only after eight years of war that the French government agreed to a referendum on Algeria's future. The result was that ninety-nine per cent of Algerians voted for independence.

Women activists who had hoped that independence would bring greater rights and freedoms for women were bitterly disappointed. Women had voting rights, but this meant little since the FLN was the only legal political party. Women protested in 1966 when the president declared that: 'Women should not be

In a detention centre in Paris Algerian women wave the FLN flag during the liberation struggle of the early 1960s.

treated equally with men in employment'. Demands for the reform of marriage and divorce laws went unheeded. Women remained second-class citizens.

INDEPENDENCE IN AFRICA

One of the last independence struggles took place in southern Africa. As other African nations were gaining independence in the 1960s, in Rhodesia the minority white settler population was tightening its grip over the majority African population. In 1965, the whites declared 'unilateral independence', despite African opposition and international protest.

Women were involved from the beginning. In 1962, African women held their first public demonstration. Although the protest was peaceful, they were arrested and sentenced to six weeks in jail or a £6 fine. Most of the women were too poor to pay the fine so they all decided to go to prison. The women's actions were reported around the world and helped to publicize African demands.

But peaceful protests were not enough. In 1972, Africans formed guerrilla armies and took to the bush from where they could launch raids on white farms and other targets. Women joined the guerrillas, at first in support roles but later in combat. By the war's end, in 1979, there were over 10,000 women soldiers. Other women supported the soldiers by cooking, hiding munitions, spying and raising funds.

In April 1980, after an election in which African women voted alongside African men, Rhodesia finally gained independence and was renamed Zimbabwe. Two years later, African women over the age of eighteen were granted rights as independent adults (they had previously been 'minors' under the guardianship of their father or husband). These moves forward symbolized their new rights as women and as a nation.

Some African women joined guerrilla armies in combat. Many more gave secret support to the fighters.

OPINION

'They put us into police jeeps and took us to prison. In a few minutes the news had spread all over the country and other women started protesting and they, too, were arrested. In Salisbury alone, over one-and-a-half thousand women were arrested, some with babies on their backs, others with children screaming.'
Sally Mugabe, Zimbabwean women's leader, 1962.

WOMEN'S LIBERATION

The 1960s saw a growing interest in women's issues in many Western countries. Shattered economies had been rebuilt and jobs were plentiful. People were open to change. Aspects of women's lives, such as education, work, marriage and children, were frequently discussed in the media and in bestselling paperbacks on psychology and childrearing. As higher education expanded, young women flocked to colleges and universities.

Nevertheless, women still earned much less than men. In 1965, women's earnings in the USA were only sixty per cent of male earnings. Most women worked in low-grade clerical and service jobs. Society regarded women's 'real work' as marriage and family.

In 1963 an American woman, Betty Friedan, published *The Feminine Mystique*, a book which explored the problems facing educated, middle-class American women. Friedan found that many were deeply unhappy with their limited roles. She argued that women were second-class citizens and urged them to find more fulfilling lives through work and education. Although her arguments were controversial, the book was an immediate success.

PROTEST MOVEMENTS

The late-1960s saw new social and political movements in many countries. In the USA, the civil rights movement, seeking equal rights for black Americans, was at its height and there was growing discontent with American involvement in the war in Vietnam. In Europe there was a new militancy among trade unions. Everywhere, growing numbers of young people – 'hippies' – were rejecting mainstream society for a freer, less materialistic lifestyle. The hippie 'alternative' culture manifested itself in music, clothes, sexual relations and the use of 'recreational' drugs. The peak year was 1968, when huge demonstrations rocked Europe and North America.

The 'hippie' culture of music and protest tried to create an alternative way of life to mainstream society.

Although many women joined protest movements, they were still not treated equally. When it came to women, many otherwise radical men held traditional views. Women were given roles not as leaders but as supporters – stuffing envelopes, making meals, turning out for marches and listening to male speeches. Some women rebelled, declaring that they were oppressed and should organize for women's rights. They were joined by other women who refused to be second-class citizens. The movement grew rapidly and called itself Women's Liberation. Eventually, it involved millions of women in many countries, rich and poor.

Chicago, 1968: protestors against American involvement in the Vietnam war are confronted by armed US guardsmen. Many women joined the anti-war movement.

THE PERSONAL IS POLITICAL

There were some similarities between the new women's movement and earlier campaigns. Like the suffragists, Women's Liberation used direct action – marches, pickets, strikes – as well as new tactics such as 'sit-ins' and 'speak-outs'. Television brought their message to an audience of millions. Some of the earlier movement's aims, such as equal pay and equal rights at work, were also championed by women's liberationists. Like the suffragists, Women's Liberation had divisions between a militant minority and a more moderate majority.

However, there were many differences between the two movements. Women's Liberation emphasized that real change must begin with women themselves, rather than the outside world. This was summed up in the phrase: 'the personal is political'. Meeting in small groups, women began to look at their lives – at how they thought and felt and why they were frustrated and angry. This 'consciousness-raising' enabled women to share experiences and support each other. In turn it led to the development of 'women-only' spaces, such as centres, bookshops and coffee-houses. For Women's Liberation, equality in personal relationships was as important as legal and political equality.

While most early women's rights campaigners had sought equality with men, Women's Liberation regarded society as deeply biased in favour of men and against women. This bias was described by the new term, 'sexist'. Women's liberationists argued that society valued women by standards set by men. There was anger at the way in which women were judged 'like cattle' in beauty contests or depicted as 'sex objects' in advertisements. Women's Liberation urged women to dress and act according to their own standards of beauty and comfort. As a result, 'women's libbers' were frequently stereotyped by

KEY MOMENT

Miss America protest
On 7 September 1968, women demonstrated against the annual Miss America contest, denouncing it as sexist and racist. People were urged to throw cosmetics, bras, corsets and women's magazines into a Freedom Trash Can to protest against women's 'high-heeled, low status' role. Media coverage was hostile but it made many women aware of the new movement.

KEY MOMENT

Strike at Ford
In 1968, women machinists at the Ford Motor factory in Dagenham, east London, UK, went on strike for equal pay for work of equal value. Although they were skilled workers, women received the lowest pay. Despite male hostility, the women stood firm. It was only after the strike brought the factory to a standstill that women's rates were raised to skilled levels. In the following years there were many more equal pay actions.

OPINION

'My liberation consists of serving him after my work while he reads or "thinks". While I peel the vegetables, he can read at leisure. Freedom only exists for the well-off ones and in the real world, the well-off one is the man.'
French socialist woman, 1969.

OPINION

'We're not beautiful, we're not ugly, we're angry.'
Protest against Miss World contest, London UK, 1970.

Beauty contests, such as Miss America, were an early target for Women's Liberation demonstrations.

their opponents as unfeminine, ugly, ill-kempt and badly dressed. Women's Liberation argued for revolutionary change. But how this change was to come about caused divisions within the movement. Some women saw the capitalist system as the reason for women's oppression and argued that only a socialist society could bring women true equality. This group developed links between Women's Liberation, trade unions and other liberation movements.

Other women argued that capitalist and socialist societies were equally sexist. They saw male power – patriarchy – as the problem and argued for a women-centred society. They led campaigns against male violence, including rape, pornography and domestic violence. These linked with campaigns for lesbian rights – some women, separatists, argued that only lesbians could be true women's liberationists since they had no sexual relations with men.

Women from minority groups suffered double discrimination – as women and as minorities. In the

Betty Friedan (above) has been involved in many aspects of women's rights, from the 1960s to the end of the century.

USA, black women played an important role in the civil rights movement. While some black women worked with white women, others chose to work separately, arguing that black women had different interests and concerns. Ethnic minority women in Europe and Canada also began separate groups. Militant women's groups also emerged in developing countries such as India and the Philippines.

THE NATIONAL ORGANIZATION OF WOMEN

Many women felt that changes could be made within the political system. In the USA, the National Organization of Women (NOW) was formed in 1966. NOW aimed to 'bring women into full participation in the mainstream of American society... in truly equal partnership with men'. NOW campaigned against unequal laws, for equal opportunities in work and education and for women in high profile positions in government and the media. While radical women saw NOW as a white, middle-class organization, as a national organization it could mobilize thousands of women. On 26 August 1970, 50,000 women marched on the fiftieth anniversary of voting rights for women.

OPINION

'Women are an oppressed class. Our oppression is total, affecting every facet of our lives. We are exploited as sex objects, breeders, domestic servants and cheap labour. We are considered inferior beings, whose only purpose is to enhance men's lives. We identify the agents of our oppression as men.' Redstockings manifesto, Women's Liberation group, New York City, USA, 1969.

A WOMAN'S RIGHT TO CHOOSE

Despite their many differences, everyone involved in the women's rights movement agreed on one vital issue – that it was a woman's right to make decisions about her body, sex and contraception. Every woman had 'a right to choose' whether, how and when she wanted children. This right belonged to her alone – not to her husband, family, employer, church or government.

Stamp of approval – the Indian government promoted contraception by suggesting that couples limit their families to a maximum of two children.

These demands came as scientific developments made safer and more reliable contraception available in many countries. The oral contraceptive pill, taken by women, was introduced in 1960. By 1966, six million women were using the pill in the USA and millions more elsewhere. In some countries, women still lacked access to contraception. For example, in France it was illegal to sell female contraceptives or provide information about contraception until 1968.

The 1960s saw changing social attitudes towards sex. Although female contraception was limited to married women, in many countries sex outside marriage was fairly common. Young women who became pregnant were sent to special homes for unmarried mothers and their babies were adopted. Unmarried mothers and their children experienced shame and discrimination.

Even with more effective contraception, there were many unwanted pregnancies. Women sought abortions to end the pregnancies. Although abortion was common it was normally illegal. In the mid-1960s, there were an estimated one million abortions every year in the USA, with between 500 and 1,000 women dying as a result of unsafe operations. Women's Liberation demanded that abortion be made legal and easily available. Demonstrations for abortion on demand took place in many countries.

The original Women's Liberation movement lasted only a few years. By the late 1970s much of the initial energy had been lost and the movement split into many different factions and campaigns. Some of its initial demands had been fulfilled, but most had not. However, the issues raised provided a solid legacy for women's rights for the rest of the century.

The right for women to have control over their own bodies is a vital one, yet it is often denied by governments. Below, a pro-abortion rally in 1989 received support from many prominent Americans.

WOMEN ENTER
THE MAINSTREAM

By the mid-1970s, women had gained the right to vote in most countries. Newly independent nations gave women voting rights. But it was only in 1971 that women in Switzerland could vote in national elections. However, even in countries where women had voted for half a century, they had often made little direct impact on political life, and women politicians were in a tiny minority. Few political parties promoted women's rights or policies important to women, such as contraception, abortion, equal pay or childcare.

Her first vote – it was not until 1971 that Swiss women could vote in national elections.

These issues began to enter mainstream politics from the 1970s, supported by well-organized women's campaigns. In the USA, NOW followed the path of the

nineteenth-century suffragists by attempting to change the US Constitution. In 1972, Congress took the first steps by accepting an Equal Rights Amendment (ERA) to guarantee equal treatment in all areas of life. In 1974, the new French government established a Ministry for Women's Rights to promote equality.

In Springfield, Illinois, thousands of women and men demonstrate in favour of the Equal Rights Amendment.

Women representing women

In Australia, the Women's Electoral Alliance organized meetings at which political candidates were asked searching questions about their policies. The Women's Electoral Alliance publicized their answers and recommended that women vote for candidates supporting women's rights. In Norway, women in political parties and women's organizations used the slogan 'women representing women' to educate women voters and encourage their involvement.

KEY MOMENT

Catholicism and divorce

Divorce was banned in Italy until 1970, when the government introduced a law permitting divorce under certain conditions. For three years the Catholic church actively campaigned to overturn the new law. Although most Italian women were Catholics, many were outraged by the church's role. In a referendum in 1974, almost sixty per cent of voters supported the new law with many more women voting in favour than men. Feminists later clashed with the church over contraception and abortion.

By the 1990s, several countries had women leaders. This is Tansu Ciller, prime minister of Turkey, in 1995.

Direct action remained important. In 1975, women in Iceland held a one-day strike to demand equal rights. Women stopped work at home and stayed away from work and school. The strike drew worldwide attention and, less than a year later, Iceland's parliament passed equal rights laws. Direct action was vital in pressing governments to change laws on controversial issues such as abortion, contraception and divorce, especially in countries where the Catholic church organized political opposition.

In some countries more women entered the political arena. During the 1970s, Norway's major political parties agreed that around thirty per cent of candidates would be women. In 1969 less than ten per cent of members of parliament were women; this had risen to twenty-four per cent by 1977 and to forty per cent by 1995, when eight out of nineteen cabinet members, and the prime minister, were women. A few women went on to political leadership in countries as various as Israel, India, the UK, Bangladesh, Pakistan, Ireland, Poland and Turkey.

However, political success did not always result in more opportunities for other women, in political life or elsewhere. Although more women than ever before were in paid work, everywhere women still earned less than men, were concentrated in 'female' jobs, and faced barriers to promotion. Cuts in welfare and social services in many countries worsened the situation of poorer women.

During the 1980s, large numbers of women camped for years outside Greenham Common military base in the UK. They were protesting against nuclear weapons held at the base.

WOMEN FOR PEACE

Many women still felt excluded from the political process. They felt that, as ever, men made the crucial decisions that affected people's lives – whether in politics, the military or multinational companies. Just as women in the 1930s had campaigned against war, so women in the 1980s brought feminism into the peace and environmental movements. Hundreds of thousands of women joined demonstrations against war and environmental destruction, as women's peace camps were set up outside military bases and nuclear establishments in Europe, Australia and North America.

In some countries, women had few opportunities to participate in political life. In the Soviet Union women had equal rights, but in practice they were far from equal. In 1970 they received only sixty-five per cent of male wages and carried the main burdens of family life. Although women were represented in parliament, real power lay with the leaders of the ruling Communist Party and these were almost always men. Protest of any sort could be punished by prison or by exile. Under these circumstances, it was difficult for women to express their views or organize for change.

THE STRUGGLE FOR HUMAN RIGHTS

This was also the case in many countries in Asia, Africa and Latin America where power was in the hands of unelected governments or military dictatorships. Neither women nor men could speak out for change without risking arrest, torture, imprisonment – and often death. Women's rights were part of the struggle for basic human rights, such as campaigns for political prisoners. Because laws were so restrictive, women often had to use direct action to draw attention to abuses.

Women have found unusual ways to highlight human rights abuses; this silent protest is being conducted by Tibetan women against Chinese rule in Tibet. Some of the worst treatment has been meted out to Buddhist nuns who have peacefully protested against Chinese occupation.

Silent dignified protest became the hallmark of a group of women in Argentina known as the Mothers of the Plaza de Mayo. These women protested in order to draw attention to their missing children, the 'disappeared', who had been taken away by soldiers and not seen or heard of since. From April 1977 onwards, the mothers of the

Like Argentinean women, women in Chile lived under a military dictatorship for many years and had to find new ways to protest. This anti-death penalty poster from 1987 reads 'Save their lives'.

'disappeared' began to gather each week in the central square in Buenos Aires. Wearing white headscarves and carrying photos of their children, they walked silently in pairs (groups of more than two people could be arrested). Despite the dangers to themselves and their families, they continued their protest for years, long after the end of military government.

By the 1990s, there were thousands of women's organizations spread over many countries. They demonstrated that women's rights was now a global movement.

WOMEN'S RIGHTS GO GLOBAL

OPINION

In 1980, halfway through the UN Decade for Women, an official UN report stated: 'Although women are fifty per cent of the world adult population, they comprise one third of the official labour force, perform nearly two thirds of all working hours, receive only one tenth of the world income, and own less than one per cent of world property.'

Women hold a 'peace torch' during the opening ceremony of the 1995 UN women's conference in Beijing, China.

In 1975, the United Nations held a women's conference to mark the start of the UN Decade for Women. This aimed to develop an international standard for women's rights. The conference was an important step in drafting a new UN Convention on the Elimination of All Forms of Discrimination Against Women and marked increased international co-operation in women's rights issues.

The first conference in Mexico City was attended by representatives of 133 governments. Here 6,000 women from non-government organizations (NGOs) made public presentations, lobbied governments and exchanged experiences. Ten years later, in Nairobi, Kenya, there were 157 governments and 15,000 NGO women. In 1995, at the women's conference in Beijing, China, there were 189 governments and 30,000 NGO women.

By bringing together women from different countries and backgrounds, the conferences demonstrated that women's rights were a global issue. But there were many different priorities and approaches. Women from Western countries saw rights mainly in terms of equal opportunities in education, employment and legal equality. African women were concerned with the effects of customary laws and practices. Many Asian women focused on the exploitation of young girls in factories and the sex industry. But there were also issues of common concern.

THE RICH-POOR DIVIDE

Poverty and its effects were dominant themes. Although many countries had experienced rising living standards, others saw increased poverty. Furthermore, the gaps between rich and poor people were increasing. Although men also suffered from poverty and lack of rights, women were especially affected, in part because of their low status in society.

In some Asian countries increasing numbers of young girls are recruited into the sex industry.

KEY MOMENT

CEDAW
The Convention on the Elimination of All Forms of Discrimination Against Women (CEDAW) was adopted by the UN in 1979 and came into force in 1981. When a government signs CEDAW it agrees to basic principles and standards to ensure equal treatment for women. CEDAW has since been signed and ratified by most of the world's governments, although some sign only parts of the document. The US government has not ratified CEDAW.

A health worker weighs a child in rural Africa. Poverty limits a child's chances for healthy development – and girls are often affected more than boys.

According to a 1995 United Nations Human Development report, about one quarter of the world's population is living in extreme poverty on an income of less than one US dollar a day. Seventy per cent of this group are women and girls, mainly in Africa, Asia and Latin America. These women lack basic social rights – such as decent housing, clean water, healthcare – as well as economic security and legal rights. They are less likely than men to own land or property or to be paid for their work, whether in agriculture, industry or the home, or to have access to credit. Many are single parents, abandoned or divorced, bringing up children alone.

Poverty leads to poor health. While most women in Western countries have access to good medical care, each year around 600,000 women in developing countries die as a result of complications in pregnancy or childbirth. Poor children are more likely to die of common childhood diseases such as diarrhoea or

50

measles, or to be sick and malnourished. Children growing up in poverty are less likely to attend school or to learn useful skills. Girls have less chance of attending school: of the world's 900 million non-literate adults, 600 million are women. Cuts in government spending on health and education affect women and girls more than men and boys.

EMPOWERMENT

Campaigners have argued that these issues need a new approach. Government action and equal rights laws have made little difference to the lives of the poorest women. What is needed is a 'bottom-up', not a 'top-down', approach. The first step is to enable poor women to decide what they want and need to improve their lives and then to work with them to find ways in which they can achieve their aims.

This process is called 'empowerment'. It bears some similarities to the 'consciousness-raising' sessions of Women's Liberation. But empowerment focuses on groups rather than individuals, and goes beyond raising awareness to taking action. An example of practical empowerment is where organizations provide access to credit to poor women. Empowerment means more than tackling poverty. It aims to raise women's low status. The process of making decisions and acting on them increases women's confidence, and helps them to overcome their isolation and powerlessness and earn the respect of others.

> ## KEY MOMENT
>
> **Women's loan scheme**
> In 1976, the Grameen (Village) Bank of Bangladesh started to make small loans to poor, rural women. These women rarely own land or property; some are divorced or abandoned. The women use the loans to buy goats or chickens or to set up as small traders, using the income for food, healthcare and their children's education. Interest rates are low and women are reliable repayers. By 1990, the Grameen Bank had one thousand branches, and similar systems had been set up in thirty other countries.

Her husband will ride the rickshaw, but it is his wife who is responsible for the Grameen Bank loan that made the new family business possible.

Many of the ideas raised by the empowerment process have been adopted by women's rights campaigners in Western countries, where women also suffer from poverty. For example, in 1980, sixty-two per cent of the USA's poorest people were women. There are many reasons why women are poorer than men: they earn less, they are more likely to work part-time, they have fewer opportunities because they care for children, and their work at home is not valued.

REPRODUCTIVE RIGHTS

Women at a family planning clinic in Indonesia discuss a female contraceptive, known as an intrauterine device (IUD).

Women at the Beijing conference also agreed on the importance of 'reproductive rights' – the right to choose whether and when to have children. To put this right into practice it was necessary for all women to have

access to safe, affordable contraception and to abortion. Access to contraception was increasing. By 1990, over half the married couples in developing countries were using modern methods of contraception, compared to less than one quarter in 1980.

However, in some countries opposition from conservative politicians or religious leaders restricts access to contraception and, especially, to abortion. Worldwide it is estimated that there are 300 million women who want to use contraceptives but cannot – either because governments will not make them available or their partners will not allow it. Poor women, young women and unmarried women are less likely to have access either to contraception or to information about sex and family planning. But some governments have tried to enforce family planning. In 1979, the Chinese government introduced a new compulsory birth control policy, the 'one-child family'. Under this policy, women must have government permission to become pregnant and those who do so without permission are forced to have an abortion.

DISCRIMINATION BEFORE BIRTH

Some societies greatly value sons over daughters. Sometimes daughters are killed shortly after birth or are deliberately neglected, receiving less food or proper care than their brothers. Sometimes discrimination occurs before birth when new technology is used to determine the sex of the fetus. The result is that many more boys are born than girls. Indian women's organizations have campaigned to end all these forms of discrimination.

Violence against women is another issue with worldwide relevance. Violence takes many forms – domestic violence in the home, rape and sexual harassment, war and conflict – but women and girls

KEY MOMENT

Putting a price on unpaid work

The 1995 UN women's conference in Beijing called on governments to find ways of measuring and valuing women's unpaid work. In 1996, the British government announced that it was commissioning surveys to determine the hours and type of women's work in the home and how it should be valued. The demand to value women's work had been raised twenty-five years earlier by Women's Liberation.

Today, most victims of war are women and children, like these Afghan refugees in Pakistan.

remain prime targets. Violence takes place in rich and poor countries – and is often considered acceptable and lawful, especially when committed by a man on his wife or child. Violence takes different forms in different countries. Women in India have campaigned against dowry deaths, whereby young brides are killed by their husband's family because they do not bring enough property into the marriage. In many countries rape crisis centres and shelters for women fleeing abusive relationships now exist. In 1993, eighty per cent of refugees assisted by United Nations agencies were women and children.

Women's sexuality and sexual expression are still controversial issues. In some countries, women and girls are punished severely for stepping outside the traditional boundaries. They may be forced into marriage (often when they are too young to give proper consent), divorced without maintenance, or deprived of their children and property – all of which may be considered normal and acceptable in their society. A largely hidden traditional practice affects over 100 million women, mainly in Africa. This is female genital mutilation – removing all or part of a girl's outer sex organs – resulting in immense health problems for girls and women. Despite great difficulties, some women's organizations and governments are trying to end the practice. In terms of women's sexual expression, no country in the world grants lesbians the same range of rights as other women, and homosexuality is illegal in some countries. For the first time at a UN gathering, the Beijing conference raised issues involving the rights of lesbians.

The 1995 women's conference in Beijing resulted in a Global Platform for Action on women's rights. This Platform contained sections on poverty, violence, education, health, work, political participation and human rights. All governments are expected to take action to make the Platform's aims a reality and to bring about equality, development and peace for all the world's women. This is the challenge for women's rights for the twenty-first century.

OPINION

'Many lesbians have been in the forefront of the struggle for women's human rights, yet women's groups have not shown equal solidarity. Whenever a lesbian's right to determine her own sexuality and to choose who to love is violated, all women's right to self-determination is weakened.' Shelley Anderson, lesbian activist, 1995.

American actors Anne Heche and Ellen Degeneres present a positive image of a lesbian couple – but discrimination and prejudice still exist.

A CENTURY OF PROGRESS?

In 1995, the United Nations attempted to measure how well women were treated worldwide. It developed a new measurement called the gender-related development index (GDI). It took statistics on health, education and living standards from each country. Then it measured whether or not women had the same opportunities for a long and healthy life, a good education and decent living conditions as men in that country.

Like other Scandinavian countries, Denmark supports working mothers by providing good quality childcare.

GDIs were calculated for 130 countries. Where the GDI was low, women had low status and few opportunities compared to men. Where the GDI was high, women had higher status and greater equality with men. It was found that no country treated its women as well as its men.

The four Scandinavian countries – Sweden, Finland, Norway and Denmark – had the highest GDIs. Here women have equal rights under the law and equal opportunities in education and at work. Government policies support working women by providing paid maternity leave, free nurseries and equal pension rights. Women are active in public life and around forty per cent of elected politicians are women.

OBSTACLES TO EQUALITY

Other Western countries, such as the USA, Canada, Australia, the UK, France and Germany, also had high GDIs. Here women had gained greater equality over the past twenty-five years; but they still encountered numerous problems. For example, women often found it difficult to combine paid work with motherhood, especially where good quality, affordable childcare was not available. And many women complained of a 'glass ceiling' which prevented them from reaching the highest positions at work. Also, while educated women were doing well, the poorest women, many from ethnic minorities, had far fewer opportunities.

In general, rich countries had higher GDIs than poor countries. But this was not always the case. Wealthy Saudi Arabia and Kuwait had low GDIs. Here women have few rights: they cannot vote, they are unequal under the law and they have restricted working opportunities. In Saudi Arabia, women are not allowed to drive cars.

On the other hand, some poorer countries had good GDI scores and were working to improve the rights of their women citizens. For example, China and Indonesia had much higher GDIs than Saudi Arabia even though they were much poorer countries. In both cases, government policies have been more favourable towards women and women's rights.

On 27 April 1994, black South African women and men wait patiently to cast their first vote in a national election.

FIGHTING POVERTY

Poverty is still a major problem for women worldwide. Poor women have fewer opportunities for education and gaining skills that might help them out of poverty. When governments cut spending on social welfare – such as benefits, housing, childcare, food subsidies and healthcare – then women are more affected than men. Women are less mobile than men – they cannot move to new work so easily because they are more likely to be responsible for the care and support of children. Supporting women's rights means fighting women's poverty worldwide.

Women in Kabul, Afghanistan, queue for food in 1996. With the Taliban in power, women are losing even the few rights they once possessed.

Sometimes women lose rights. After the collapse of Communism in the former Soviet Union in the late 1980s, unemployment rose rapidly. A Russian government minister said: 'Why should we employ women when men are unemployed?' In Russia more women are losing their jobs and their right to free childcare, education and unemployment benefit. In

Afghanistan, the country with the very lowest GDI score, women are losing even the few rights they possessed. The Taliban – the men in control of the country – will not allow women to be educated, to do paid work or take part in public life. Women who do not obey are beaten.

ORGANIZING FOR CHANGE

This book has looked at the achievements of women, and the rights they have gained during the twentieth century. It has studied the ways in which outside forces – such as wars, economic conditions and scientific developments – have shaped women's lives, for better or worse. It has discussed the importance of ideas, and the politics that put ideas into action. Above all, it has shown how women have become aware of their rights and learnt to express and organize themselves to achieve these rights.

Over the century, women have gained more rights than ever before. No country has yet reached true equality between women and men but most have taken real and important steps towards building a more equal and just society.

KEY MOMENT

The Women's Coalition
Women have been prominent in civil rights and peace movements during thirty years of conflict in Northern Ireland (1968-98). In 1997, the Women's Coalition was formed by Catholic and Protestant women from most sections of society in Northern Ireland, including the women's movement, trade unions and community organizations. Two representatives were elected to the peace talks of 1997-8 where they played an important role in bridging gaps between the main parties and promoting equality for all citizens. In June 1998 two representatives were elected to the Northern Ireland Assembly.

Happy, healthy, equal at home and at work – a goal for all women in the twenty-first century.

GLOSSARY

abortion ending a pregnancy (usually in the first few months).

allied countries (in the Second World War) countries opposing Germany, Japan and Italy – mainly Britain and Commonwealth countries, the USA and the Soviet Union.

birth control the use of contraception to prevent pregnancy and limit family size.

boycott the breaking off of trade links with a country, or the refusal to take part in an action, as a form of protest.

capitalism an economic system based on the private ownership of land and industry, in which most people work for wages.

citizenship having the status of a citizen, i.e. belonging to a country and having and using rights as a citizen (for example, the right to vote, to speak freely etc.).

civil service the service responsible for the public administration of the government of a country.

civil war a war within a country.

Communist parties political parties claiming to support working-class people – usually through revolution and government control of the economy.

constitution a document that sets out the principles and standards for a country's government.

contraception the prevention of a pregnancy (through use of contraceptives, e.g. condoms, the pill etc.).

covenant a binding legal document.

Depression (of the 1930s) an economic downturn with massive unemployment.

direct action campaigns co-ordinated activities, e.g. demonstrations, pickets, marches, which influence people and governments.

disarmament the giving up by a country of all or some of its military weapons.

empower to give people (in this case, women) power over their own lives.

'female jobs' jobs done mainly by women, and seen as women's work.

feminist a women who believes in and works for women's rights.

fetus the developed embryo in the womb.

guerrilla armies resistance forces, usually working in small groups, attacking better equipped enemy forces.

hunger strike going without food as a deliberate means of protest.

hyper-inflation an economic situation in which money loses value very quickly.

Labour parties socialist parties in Britain, Australia and New Zealand.

lesbians women who are sexually attracted to and have sexual relations with other women.

literacy the ability to read and write.

literate able to read and write.

lobby a group of people working to make a government or organization change its laws and practices.

militant aggressive or vigorous, especially in the support of a cause.

nationalism loyalty to one's country above others, sometimes involving a struggle to free one's country from foreign domination.

nationalist a person who believes in nationalism.

polling booth a semi-enclosed cubicle in which people vote during elections.

pornography writings, pictures, films etc. with detailed sexual descriptions or images.

radical favouring ideas or actions that are different from those generally accepted.

referendum a vote on an important issue.

refugee a person forced to leave their country because of violence or persecution.

'Rights of Man' a declaration of political rights made during the French Revolution (1789-99); 'Men are born free and equal in rights...'.

service industry an industry that provides services, such as transport or entertainment, rather than goods.

socialist parties political parties supporting working-class people and working for gradual change through parliament, rather than revolution.

stereotype a widely shared notion that all members of a particular social group have the same (usually negative) characteristic.

suffrage the right to vote in elections.

suffragette a suffragist who mainly relied on direct action to win women's right to vote.

suffragist a person campaigning for women's right to vote.

trade union an organization of workers campaigning for better wages and conditions.

unilateral an action taken without consulting others.

United Nations an international organization, founded in 1945 to maintain world peace and promote human rights.

white-collar jobs jobs in service industries.

BOOKS TO READ

Advocacy Kit on the Convention on the Elimination of All Forms of Discrimination Against Women, UNIFEM/UNICEF, 1995.
Contains five booklets and nine information sheets on CEDAW. It also looks at the links between CEDAW and the Child Rights Convention.

A Century of Women - The History of Women in Britain and the United States by Sheila Rowbotham, Viking, 1997, Penguin, 1999.
An accessible and readable decade-by-decade account of the experiences of British and American women, drawing out similarities and differences between them.

'Dare to be Free' and Justice at the Door! The Struggle for Women's Equality (1830-1930), both by Jean Holder and Katherine Milcoy, Fawcett Library, 1997/8.
The first pack focuses on the fight for the vote and the second looks at broader issues including marriage, family and work. Both packs contain images, text and teacher's notes and are UK-focused. There is a separate pack for younger children.

Emmeline Pankhurst by Michael Pollard (Tell Me About It series), Evans Brothers, 1996.
An illustrated history for younger readers.

Feminism for Beginners by Susan Watkins, Marisa Rueda and Mata Rodriguez, Icon Books, 1992.
A lively, illustrated history of feminism from a radical viewpoint.

Feminism for Teenagers by Sophie Grillet, Piccadilly Press, 1997.
Organized into sections on domesticity, work, politics, violence and rights, and illustrated with cartoons.

Gender Issues by Kaye Stearman and Nikki van der Gaag (Global Issues series), Wayland, 1995.
Women's and men's roles in many cultures and how they have changed.

Human Development Report 1995, United Nations Development Programme, 1995.
This report attempts to measure gender equality worldwide and suggests national and international action for women's rights.

India Fights Colonialism, LONDEC, 1995.
Focuses on the role of women in the Nationalist movement.

Indira Gandhi by Kathryn Marshall (Women Achievers series), Exley, 1997.
With background material and photos.

It's About Time: Human Rights are Women's Right, Amnesty International, 1995.
Published to launch Amnesty International's 1995 campaign on women's rights. It highlights the situation of women in seventy-five countries.

Let's Discuss Women's Rights by Barbara Einhorn (Let's Discuss series), Wayland, 1988.
Looks at work, education, contraception, sexual harassment. Includes UK case studies.

100 Greatest Women by Michael Pollard, Dragon's World, 1995.
Includes political leaders and women's rights campaigners from many countries.

People's Century edited by Godfrey Hodgson, BBC Books, 1995/6, two volumes.
A twentieth-century history drawing on personal testimony from ordinary women and men. There is an accompanying video series.

Solid Ground edited by Jane Leggett and Sue Libovitch, Unwin Hyman Collections.
Writings by women from around the world, including Ireland, South Africa, Egypt and USA, with follow-on activities.

The State of Women in the World Atlas by Joni Seager, Penguin Reference, 1997.
Facts and figures on women's lives today in brightly illustrated maps and tables.

The Suffragettes in Pictures by Diana Atkinson, Museum of London, 1996.
Photos, posters and words from 1900 to 1920.

A Woman's Place: The Changing Picture of Women in Britain by Diana Souhami, Penguin Books, 1986.
Facts, quotes and statistics with accompanying photos cover suffragettes, women in wartime and women's life in the mid-1980s.

Weighing Up the Evidence series, Dryad Press, 1988.
Includes *Women and Power*, women's place in history, from ancient times to the present – largely UK based.

Women and World Development series, Zed Books, 1990s.
Information books. Includes *Women and Human Rights, Refugee Women, Women and Health* and *Women and Work*.

Women History Makers series, Macdonald's Children's Books.
Includes *Solidarity*, an historical account of three women's rights campaigners from the UK, Japan and the USA.

Women in History series, Cambridge University Press, 1988-9.
Titles include *Votes for Women, On All Fronts: Women in the First World War, Women in Revolutionary Russia* and *Keep Smiling Through; Women in the Second World War.*

Women in History series, Wayland, 1989-91.
Includes *Women and Education, Women and the Family, Women and Politics* and *Women and Work.*

Women Making History series, BT Batsford, 1991.
Includes *Women at Work, Women in World War Two* and *Black Women in Britain.*

GAMES

Who is She?, London Union of Youth Clubs, Girl's Fund, 64 Camberwell Road, London SE5 0EN, UK, 1993.
A board-game about women's history around the world.

VIDEOS

The Moving Pictures Bulletin, issue 24, March 1998.
Focuses on women's rights worldwide, with articles and video lists. (Available from Television Trust for the Environment, TVE Centre, Prince Albert Road, London NW2 4RZ, UK.)

AMNESTY INTERNATIONAL

Amnesty International UK, 99-119 Rosebery Avenue, London EC1R 4RE
Internet address: http://www.amnesty.org.uk/

Amnesty International has over one million members and supporters in some 150 countries throughout the world who contribute to its work. Members work within a closely defined mandate:
- To seek the release of prisoners of conscience – those imprisoned solely for their beliefs, colour, sex, ethnic origin, language or religion who have not used or advocated the use of violence.
- To work for fair and prompt trials for all political prisoners.
- To oppose the death penalty, torture, and other cruel, inhuman or degrading treatment or punishment of all prisoners.
- To end extrajudicial executions and 'disappearances'.

Amnesty International also works:
- Against abuses by opposition groups, such as hostage-taking; torture and killing of prisoners and other arbitrary killings.
- For asylum seekers who are at risk of being returned to a country where they might be held as prisoners of conscience, 'disappear', or suffer torture or execution.
- For people who are forced to leave their country because of the peaceful expression of their beliefs, or because of their ethnic origin, sex, colour or language.

Amnesty International Youth Action Network
Youth Action is the youth movement of Amnesty International, made up of around 10,000 young people. The majority are involved in one of Amnesty's Youth Action groups. They receive action magazines and newsletters and are involved in campaign activities, including human rights concerts, letter-writing, street art and cafe-crawls.

You can contact Amnesty Youth Action at the main address, or e-mail: student@amnesty.org.uk

USEFUL ADDRESSES

The following organizations are likely to provide either further information or educational material for young people and their teachers.

AUSTRALIA

Australian Council for Overseas Aid (ACFOA)
Private Bag 3, Deakin, ACT 2601
Community Aid Abroad
156 George St, Fitzroy, Melbourne, Victoria 3065
Human Rights and Equal Opportunities Commission
PO Box 5218, Sydney, NSW 2001
Office of the Status of Women
Department of the Prime Minister and Cabinet, 3-5 National Circuit, Barton, ACT 2600
The Women's Bureau
Department of Employment, Education, Training and Youth Affairs, GPO Box 9880, Canberra, ACT 2601

CANADA

Canadian Advisory Council on the Status of Women/Association Canadienne pour l'advancement des Femmes du Canada
PO Box 2000, Charlottetown, Prince Edward Island C1A 7N8
National Action Committee on the Status of Women
Suite 203, 234 Eglington Ave East, Toronto, Ontario M4P 1K5
Oxfam Canada
251 Laurier Ave West, Ottawa, Ontario KIP 5J6

NEW ZEALAND

CORSO
PO Box 9716, Wellington
Human Rights Commission
PO Box 5045, Lambton Quay. 8th Floor, Vogel Building, Aitken St, Thorndon, Wellington
Ministry of Women's Affairs
48 Mulgrave St, Box 10049, Wellington

REPUBLIC OF IRELAND

Department of Equality and Law Reform
33-39 Mespil Road, Dublin 4

Trocaire (Catholic Agency for World Development)
169 Booterstown Ave, Blackrock, Co. Dublin

UK

Christian Aid
PO Box 100, London SE1 7RT
Department for International Development (DFID)
Eland House, Stag Place, London SW1E 5DH
Equal Opportunities Commission
Overseas House, Quay St, Manchester M3 3HN
National Library of Women (Fawcett Library)
London Guildhall University, Old Castle St, London E1 7NT
National Association of Development Education Centres (NADEC)
6 Endsleigh St, London WC1H 0DS
Oxfam Supporter Services
274 Banbury Rd, Oxford OX2 7DZ
Scottish Education and Action for Development (SEAD)
23 Castle St, Edinburgh EH2 3DN, Scotland
WOMANKIND Worldwide
122 Whitechapel St, London E1 7PT

USA

International Women's Tribune Centre
777 United Nations Plaza, New York, NY 10017
Oxfam America
115 Broadway, Boston MA 02116
UN Development Fund for Women (UNIFEM)
304 East 45th St, 1106, New York, NY 10017
National Organization of Women (NOW)
1000 16th St, Ste 700, Washington, DC 20036
United Nations Division for the Advancement of Women
2 United Nations Plaza, DC2-12th Floor, New York, NY 10017
Women's Environment and Development Organization (WEDO)
355 Lexington Ave, New York, NY 10017

INDEX